THE CREATION OF

CAPTAIN AMERICA®

THOMAS FORGET

The Rosen Publishing Group, Inc.,
New York

To the King

Published in 2007 by The Rosen Publishing Group, Inc.
29 East 21st Street, New York, NY 10010

First Edition

Thanks to Marvel Entertainment, Inc.: Avi Arad, James Hinton, Mary Law, Bruno Maglione, Tim Rothwell, Mickey Stern, Alberta Stewart, and Carl Suecoff

Library of Congress Cataloging-in-Publication Data

Forget, Thomas.
Captain America/Thomas Forget.
   p. cm.—(Action Heroes)
ISBN 1-4042-0766-X (lib. bndg.)
1. America, Captain (Fictitious character) I. Title. II. Series.
PN6728.C35F67 2006
741.5'973—dc22

                                                   2005032024

Manufactured in the United States of America

On the cover: Captain America leaps into action in this illustration by co-creator Jack Kirby.

38179000659118

CONTENTS

INTRODUCTION 5

1 THE CAPTAIN'S CO-CREATORS 7

2 AMERICA'S SUPER-SOLDIER 15

3 CAP SOLDIERS ON 22

4 THE LIVING LEGEND 30

TIMELINE: JOE SIMON AND JACK KIRBY 40

CAPTAIN AMERICA HIGHLIGHTS 41

GLOSSARY 42

FOR MORE INFORMATION 43

FOR FURTHER READING 44

BIBLIOGRAPHY 46

INDEX 47

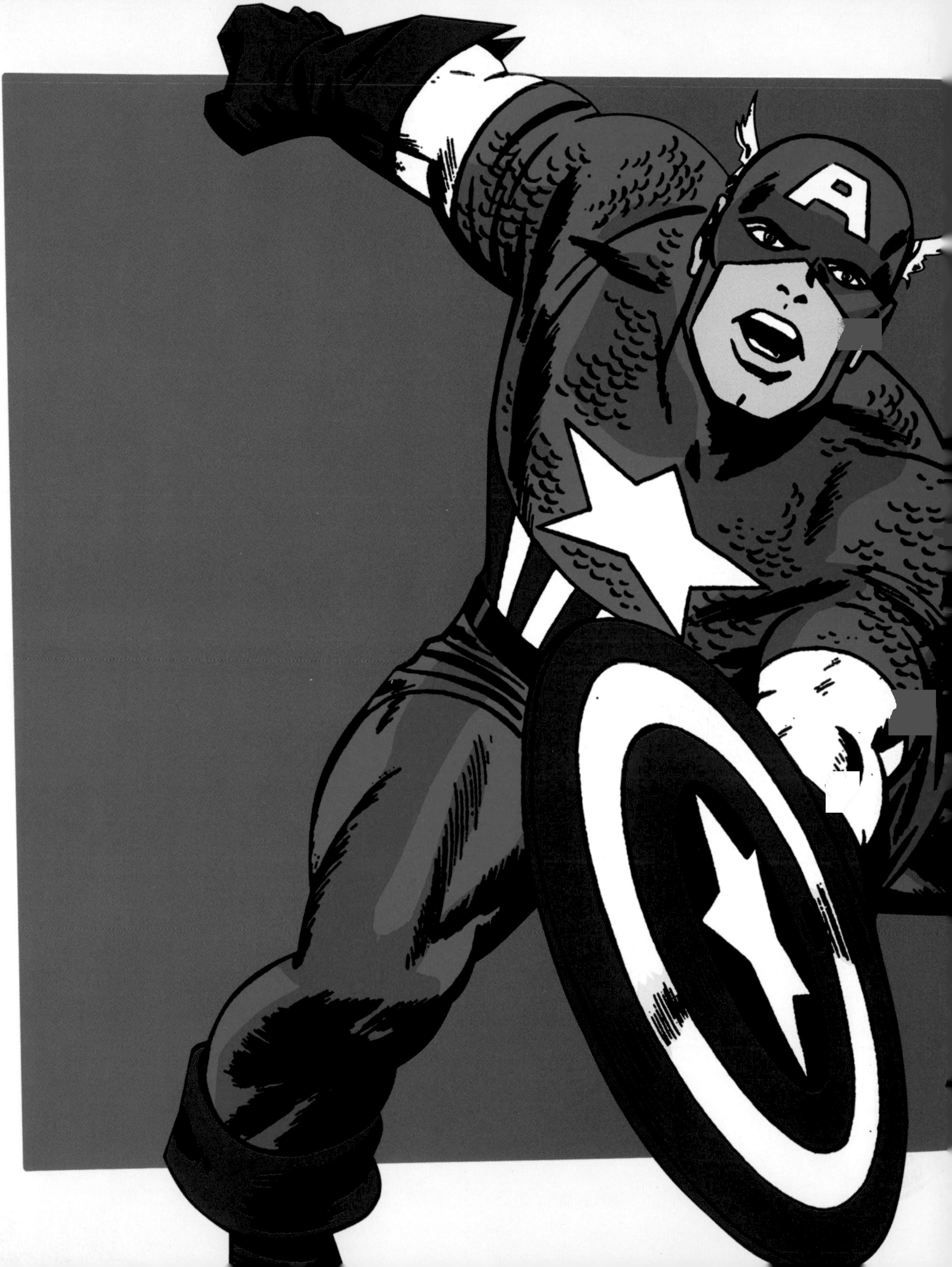

INTRODUCTION

Whenever tyrants have threatened the Marvel Universe, one hero has sprung into action. Like a living, breathing American flag, he leaps into the mouth of danger with only his wits, guts, and colorful shield to protect him. The hero is Captain America, and since 1940, he has been a familiar face on the comic book page.

Captain America is a rarity in the world of comics. Unlike many comic book heroes, he lacks superhuman powers. The serum that transformed him did not make him invulnerable or superstrong. Instead, it elevated him to the very peak of human potential. He is as fast, strong, and athletic as a human being can possibly be. But what makes Cap a true hero are the heart and mind that drive his perfect body.

Over the years, dozens of talented men and women have chronicled his adventures. In the beginning, however, he was created by two talented kids who were determined to lift themselves out of the Great Depression. One of them, Joe Simon, came from upstate New York. The other, Jack Kirby, rose out of the gritty streets of the Lower East Side, in New York City. Both of these men would go on to co- create entire worlds of characters and leave their stamp on many others. But Captain America was the creation that made them famous.

Captain America elevated a struggling comic book company, Timely, to great heights. Eventually, Timely would become the powerhouse Marvel Comics Group. Marvel is now one of America's largest and most admired comics publishers. There are only a few comic book Super Heroes who can be recognized even by people who do not regularly read comics. Captain America belongs to this club.

1 THE CAPTAIN'S CO-CREATORS

Marvel Comics made its mark with stories based in New York City. So it is only fitting that the real-life story of Captain America's co-creators begins in the Big Apple. Jacob Kurtzberg was born on August 28, 1917. His family lived in New York's tough Lower East Side. Jacob was a lot like other kids in the neighborhood, crammed into a tiny tenement with his family. The Kurtzbergs had very little money, but they did what they could to get by.

Jacob understood that he was no use to his family by being idle. So, from a young age, he began running errands for newspapermen. On weekends, he would treat himself to gangster and science fiction movies. The bold adventures depicted in these early motion pictures provided him with an escape from the drabness of his neighborhood. Young Jacob dreamed of getting away to Hollywood and becoming an actor. Unfortunately, the grim reality of his situation was always present. The Lower East Side was infested with street gangs. Any kid not tough enough to run with a gang was a target. At twelve years old, Jacob often found himself forced to defend his younger brother, David, from crowds of bullies. Jacob's hatred of bullies stuck with him throughout his life.

The violence of the neighborhood got to Jacob. He often thought of becoming just like the well-dressed gangsters who roamed the Lower East Side. As he explained years later, fighting was a common everyday occurrence. It became second nature to him, and he even began to like it. The fighting spirit never really left him, but he did eventually discover a better way to channel it.

A WAY OUT

Things began to change for Jacob when he discovered a magazine in a gutter. It was an issue of *Wonder Stories*, with a cover featuring a rocket ship. He had never seen a rocket before, and he was amazed. Jacob began seeking out other printed adventures, eventually discovering newspaper strips like Hal Foster's *Prince Valiant*. The beautifully drawn *Valiant* strip was unlike anything he had ever seen in a newspaper. It looked more like classic illustration. Jacob was hooked. The next step was for him to create comics of his own.

Jacob Kurtzberg is shown working on a cover of *Tales of Suspense* in 1965. By that time, Kurtzberg was better known as Jack Kirby. Kirby, who co-created Captain America with Joe Simon, also had a hand in co-creating an entire universe of Marvel Comics Super Heroes with writer Stan Lee. When this photo was taken, Kirby was working on some of Marvel's most popular characters, including Thor, the Fantastic Four, and Captain America.

Unfortunately, a lack of money made him abandon his dream of studying art. However, Jacob taught himself how to draw by carefully analyzing the newspaper strips

By 1936, Jacob was ready to try making a living as an artist. First, he found work with a newspaper company. Later, he landed in Max Fleischer's animation studio, where artists worked on many popular cartoons. At the studio, Jacob was an "in-betweener" on Popeye cartoons. For this job, he drew the steps in between the characters'

9

Hal Foster's *Prince Valiant* comic strip (shown above) began running in newspapers in 1937. Foster's style inspired countless other artists at the time, among them Jack Kirby. With its fine detail and draftsmanship, the *Prince Valiant* strip opened the doors of artistic imagination and influenced the Super Hero comics explosion of the early 1940s.

main movements. It was a living, but to Jacob it seemed a little too much like an assembly line. Soon, however, the comic strip landscape would change with the arrival of a certain super character from the planet Krypton.

THE REIGN OF SUPERMAN

Toward the end of the 1930s, a whole new form of entertainment began popping up all over the United States. Comic books, as they were called, were a new, inexpensive way for kids to get a lot of exciting strips in one place. The first comics were reprints of older strips that were bound together and sold for a reasonable price. Often, these books were sixty-four pages for a dime. These early comic books sold pretty well, but the invention of one special character would soon create the modern comic book we know today.

Superman was created by Jerry Siegel and Joe Schuster. Siegel and Schuster were two shy, intelligent, Jewish teens from Cleveland, Ohio. Their hero first appeared in National Periodical Publications' *Action Comics* #1 (June 1938). It sold more than 900,000 copies. This was incredible because most successful comics at that time sold between 200,000 and 400,000 copies. Suddenly, publishers everywhere wanted to write adventures for their own Superman. In New York, Jacob Kurtzberg found himself working in a booming business, with many new opportunities opening up to him.

Kurtzberg eventually moved to the legendary comic book workshop of Will Eisner. Eisner was a pioneer in full-length graphic novels. Among other strips, he created the groundbreaking comic strip called *The Spirit*. Eisner co-owned the shop with Jerry Iger. Together, they led a team of artists and writers who banged out comic books for other companies to publish. Kurtzberg began using different pseudonyms for his work at this time. These names included Jack Cortez, Jack Curtiss, and the one that stuck, Jack Kirby. Like many children of immigrants, Kurtzberg yearned to be a part of America. These invented names had an all-American feel that gave him a sense of pride.

A FATEFUL MEETING

After working with Eisner and Iger, Kurtzberg next worked at Fox Features Syndicate, owned by Victor Fox. While Kurtzberg was working there, a man named Joe Simon came to fill the position of

Joe Simon *(right)* poses with longtime Fantastic Four inker Joe Sinnott at a comics convention. In addition to co-creating Captain America, Simon was a pioneer in the genre of romance comics. He also worked on such popular DC Comics characters as Manhunter and Sandman. Simon's early work at Timely Publications (later Marvel Comics) helped make Marvel the powerhouse it is today.

artist and editor. With Simon's arrival, Captain America's "parents" were finally joined together.

Joe Simon's background was similar to Kurtzberg's in some ways, but worlds apart in others. Simon was born in Rochester, in upstate New York. Like Kurtzberg, he was the son of a tailor. Simon, however, was raised in a middle-class environment. Both young men were Jewish, with family ties to eastern Europe. But while Kurtzberg knew very little about life outside of the Lower East Side, Simon was more worldly. He knew how to use attorneys when negotiating a freelance contract. This put him in a better bargaining position than many of the other men in the early comics field. These others, like Jacob Kurtzberg, often came from such poor backgrounds that they would take whatever deal they were offered, even if it was unfair.

Simon worked for a while as a newspaper art director in Syracuse, New York. He had been supporting his family since he was eighteen. Then, in 1938, he moved to New York City to begin his first job in comics. He started out with First Funnies, Inc. This company created and delivered whole comics for publishers that did not want to hire their own editorial staffs. One of First Funnies' biggest clients was a publisher named Martin Goodman. Goodman published inexpensive magazines called pulps, but he realized there was a lot of money to be made in comics. Instead of "reinventing the wheel," Goodman looked to recreate the success of Superman with similar comic book heroes.

THE MARVEL AGE

By the end of summer 1939, Goodman's Timely Publications was in the comic book business. It soon released *Marvel Comics* #1, with a cover date of October 1939. (The issue probably hit the newsstands a month or two earlier.) This first issue provided Goodman and Timely with a big hit. *Marvel Comics* #1 featured such characters as Carl Burgos's Human Torch and Bill Everett's Sub-Mariner. Its popularity positioned Timely as a solid competitor to National Periodical Publications, the industry leader better known as DC Comics.

Joe Simon happened to be working as a freelance artist and editor at Timely when that company's influence started to grow. While working at Timely, Simon co-created new characters such as Fiery Mask, a crime fighter who could shoot flames from his eyes. But Simon did not work just for Timely. He also took a job as artist and editor at Fox Features Syndicate, where he met Jacob Kurtzberg.

Later in 1939, Martin Goodman decided that he needed his own staff. Goodman was impressed with the work Joe Simon had done for him at Timely, so he hired the talented young man to be his first staff editor. Simon's main job was to develop new characters. Within a year, Kurtzberg joined Simon as a full-time art director.

TRIAL AND ERROR

About this time, Kurtzberg legally changed his name to Jack Kirby. In their first year together, Simon and Kirby created many new "supermen" for Timely. Most of them flopped, appearing in a few issues and then vanishing forever. One of them, the Red Raven, made only one appearance. A minor success was a character called the Vision. This was a mysterious being from another dimension who traveled to Earth in clouds of smoke. Simon and Kirby later said their cigar-smoking habits inspired the Vision.

Such characters as the Sub-Mariner and the Human Torch attracted new readers. However, these Timely titles were not as widely read as Superman, Batman, and Wonder Woman over at DC Comics. Martin Goodman wanted still more popular characters. Joe Simon finally came up with an idea for a new character that he was certain would sell. He quickly sketched out a colorful uniform of red, white, and blue. It was a lot like Superman's uniform, but it was patterned after the American flag. He sent the sketch to Goodman with a note attached. It said: "Martin—Here's the character. I think he should have a kid buddy or he'll be talking to himself all the time. I'm working up a script—send schedule." This new character was Captain America.

2 AMERICA'S SUPER-SOLDIER

Captain America's arrival came at a time when the world was in turmoil. In Europe, Italy was under the leadership of Fascist dictator Benito Mussolini. On September 1, 1939, German leader Adolf Hitler invaded Poland with his Nazi armies, signaling the beginning of World War II. At the same time, Japan was at war with China. The three powers—Italy, Germany, and Japan— formed a partnership called the Axis. European nations like Great Britain and France fought hard to keep the Nazis from invading their territories, but things were not going well. The question on everyone's mind was whether the United States would get involved.

Back in the United States, President Franklin Delano Roosevelt was determined to keep his nation out of the conflict. Many Americans did not want to get involved in another war so soon after the devastating First World War (1914–1918). For a large segment of the population, however, it was frustrating to watch Hitler take control of more and more territory. Hitler's policies were especially harsh for European Jews, so for Jewish Americans in particular, it was painful to see America stand by without acting.

As Jews whose families had only recently come to America, Simon, Kirby, and Martin Goodman were all deeply concerned with what was happening overseas. Hitler's racist policies enraged them. In fact, they had Timely characters like the Human Torch and Sub-Mariner fighting the Nazis long before the United States took up arms against them in reality. Hitler's continuing march across Europe gave Jack Kirby and Joe Simon a bold idea. While thinking up Captain America, they were also looking for a villain. They recognized a bully when they saw one, and Adolf Hitler fit the bill.

Timely made plans to introduce Captain America to the public. Usually, a new character was introduced in one of Timely's existing titles, such as *Marvel Mystery Comics*. But Simon and Kirby premiered Captain America in a first issue of his own title. At the time,

Captain America Comics #1. The bold, attention-grabbing cover for Captain America's first issue came at a time when America was not yet at war with Nazi Germany. The controversial cover set the tone for the character's patriotic exploits. As long as World War II raged, Cap's enemies were almost always Nazis. Once the war was over, however, his creators had a hard time finding enemies that matched up to these real-life opponents.

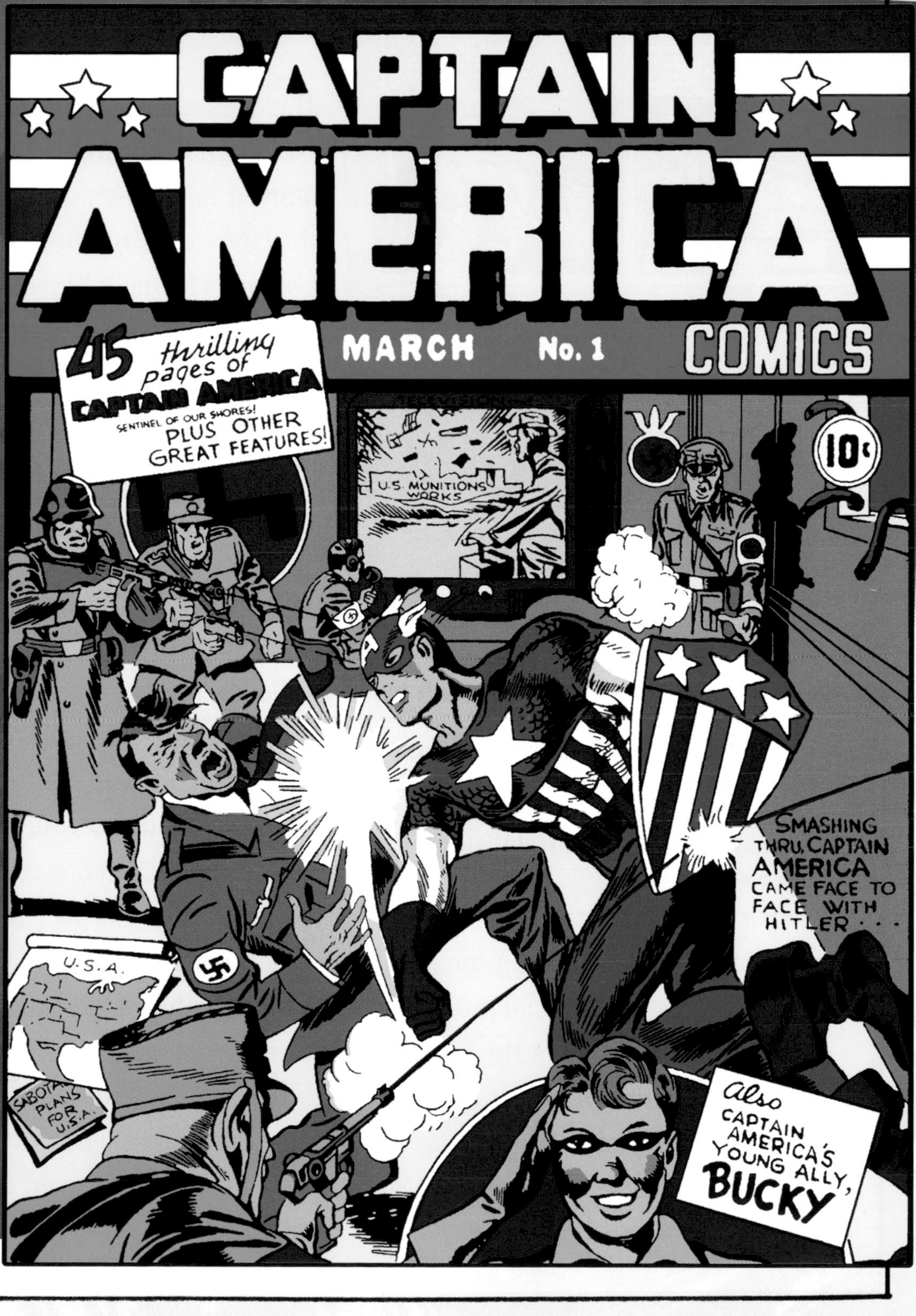
CAPTAIN AMERICA COMICS
MARCH No. 1
10¢
45 thrilling pages of CAPTAIN AMERICA SENTINEL OF OUR SHORES! PLUS OTHER GREAT FEATURES!
U.S. MUNITIONS WORKS
SMASHING THRU, CAPTAIN AMERICA CAME FACE TO FACE WITH HITLER . . .
U.S.A.
SABOTAGE PLANS FOR U.S.A.
also CAPTAIN AMERICA'S YOUNG ALLY, BUCKY

Captain America's transformation origi-
nally appeared in the first issue of
Captain America. Here, it is seen redrawn
by Kirby for a 1965 issue of *Tales of
Suspense*. Unlike Superman or the Sub-
Mariner, Cap was not born with his
powers. Instead, he received them through
science. For many children in America,
seeing skinny Steve Rogers turn into mus-
cular Captain America mirrored their own
wishes to be powerful.

this was almost unheard of. Not even Superman had started in his own comic! On the cover of *Captain America Comics* #1, the bold red, white, and blue Captain is seen delivering a devastating knockout punch to Adolf Hitler himself.

CAP COMES TO LIFE

On the pages of the first issue of *Captain America*, readers thrilled to the story of Steve Rogers. Rogers is a frail, young New Yorker who wants very badly to volunteer for the U.S. Army. He is turned down, however, because of his poor physical condition. Fortunately for him, he gets a second chance when he is offered a slot in a special program designed to create a super-soldier.

Rogers swallows the Super-Soldier serum and is transformed into a physically perfect human being. Just as this triumph takes place, however, a Nazi agent assassinates the scientist who developed the serum, Professor Erskine. With the formula lost forever, Steve Rogers becomes one of a kind.

Rogers is given a colorful costume and the name Captain America. In addition to the costume, Rogers receives a triangular shield. (Later, it would be replaced with a round one that he could hurl like a discus.) The government also fixes up Rogers with a special cover as a bungling private in the army. To his fellow soldiers, Steve Rogers is just a "grunt" like them, holed up in fictional Camp Lehigh.

For Cap to be complete, one more puzzle piece was needed. As Simon had said in his letter, Cap needed someone to talk to. That someone turns out to be Camp Lehigh's mascot, James Buchanan "Bucky" Barnes. Bucky is a youth who accidentally discovers that Steve Rogers and Captain America are the same man. Bucky and Cap strike a bargain: Bucky agrees not to reveal Cap's true identity as long as he can become Cap's partner.

CAPTAIN AMERICA'S SHIELD

Captain America's shield is one of the most recognizable accessories in comics. In his first appearance, Cap used a triangular shield with stars and stripes. But MLJ Comics (later called Archie Comics) claimed Cap's triangle shield looked too much like the chest insignia of their successful patriotic hero, the Shield. Martin Goodman asked Simon and Kirby to change it to the round shield that we know today.

Like Cap himself, his shield is one of a kind. It is an indestructible blend of the fictional metals vibranium and adamantium. Since receiving the shield, Captain America has parted ways with it only a few times. During one period, an energy shield replaced it. Cap's original shield, however, always comes back.

STAR-SPANGLED SUCCESS

The first issue of *Captain America* was a smash. Jam-packed with adventure, it sold a million copies. It was cover-dated March 1941, although it first went on sale in December 1940. In the first issue, Cap is created and begins fighting anti-American menaces. These include his future archenemy, the terrifying Red Skull. With the comic's success, Timely found itself on the same level as power-house DC Comics.

Cap's continued popularity was helped along by history. Having the new hero pose as an army private was a stroke of genius. America was on the verge of entering World War II (1939–1945), and many of the young men who read the *Captain America* comic would soon become privates themselves.

Captain America's popularity was enhanced because of how different he was physically from most of the other comic book heroes of the time. Unlike Superman or Captain Marvel, he is not all-powerful and invulnerable. Unlike Batman, he is not a millionaire. In fact, Cap has no superpowers at all. The Super-Soldier serum allows him to become a perfect human, but he is still merely human. He can easily be injured by knives and guns. On the real battle-fields, ordinary men performed heroic acts every day. In light of this, Cap's humanity was a powerful thing indeed. A huge number of the young soldiers who were sent abroad to fight in World War II remained Captain America fans.

AN ORPHANED CAP

Captain America was a great success, but Simon and Kirby were not satisfied with the treatment they received at Timely. Simon had a handshake agreement with Martin Goodman for 25 percent of the profits on *Captain America*. When Simon felt that he and his partner were not getting their fair share, he began meeting with the owners of rival DC Comics. The bosses at Timely found out about the meetings and were furious. Late in 1941, after almost a year of working on the *Captain America* title, Simon and Kirby were asked to leave the company. As soon as their last issue of *Captain America* was finished, the writing team went directly to DC Comics. Kirby would return to write *Captain America*, but not for a long time.

At Timely, Martin Goodman suddenly found himself without his art director and editor. He had to give the job of writing *Captain America* to the only man left. This was young Stanley "Stan Lee" Lieber. Lieber was the cousin of Goodman's wife. While he may not have known it at the time, Stan Lee would be associated with Captain America for decades.

On December 7, 1941, Japan bombed Pearl Harbor, bringing America into World War II. Soon, many young men were being shipped overseas to defend the United States. Beginning in 1943, Joe Simon and Jack Kirby themselves would serve in the military. Patriotism swelled, and *Captain America* became more popular than ever.

3 CAP SOLDIERS ON

As long as Americans fought in World War II, Captain America remained a popular and relevant character. In 1945, however, the war came to a close. As America and its allies emerged victorious, Cap seemed to be a character without a purpose. Young Stan Lee devised special gimmicks to juice up sales, but they did not work. For instance, he had Bucky shot and replaced him with a new girl sidekick, Golden Girl. Lee also had Cap discharged from the army to return to a job teaching school. *Captain America* limped along with stories like these until February 1950, when the series was cancelled. By then, Cap was not even the star of his own book. It had been retitled

Captain America's Weird Tales and it featured mostly horror and crime stories.

CAP VS. THE COMMIES

In the late 1940s, Timely became known as Atlas Comics. The company struggled to ride the waves in comic trends, publishing horror, science fiction, westerns, and romance comics. Would a patriotic comic book like *Captain America* ever be popular again? Time would tell.

As a result of World War II, the Communist Soviet Union became a world power. The Soviet brand of Communism was supposed to be a system in which everyone shared the wealth. Soviet society was intended to be fair and balanced. However, under brutal dictator Josef Stalin, the people of the Soviet Union found their freedoms severely restricted. What was worse, Soviet-style Communism was spreading to other countries.

Even on American soil, Communism was thought to be widespread. In 1950, Senator Joseph McCarthy of Wisconsin dropped a bombshell. He made wild claims that he had a list of Communists working in the U.S. State Department. McCarthy never backed up the claims, but his accusations were enough to scare people all over the country. Suddenly it seemed like anyone, even your next-door neighbor, could be a Communist spy.

These historical developments gave Stan Lee good ideas for reviving Cap for a new audience. Since his debut in 1939, Captain America was thought of as the first line of defense against threats to the American way of life. So, in 1954, Captain America returned in his new role for issue #76: Captain America . . . Commie Smasher!

The new adventures were drawn by future Spider-Man artist John Romita and mostly written by Stan Lee. However, despite the efforts of these talented men, the new stories did not click with the public. After just three issues, Captain America was cancelled again. He was not the only hero to fall. All over the comics industry, Super Heroes were losing popularity. In their place, intelligent but gory horror titles were selling like hotcakes. At this time, Joe Simon and Jack Kirby were working on successful romance comics. The duo even founded their own company, Mainline Comics. The classic Super Hero was simply vanishing from the comic racks.

COMICS ON THE ROPES

From their very beginning, comic books were criticized for their unwholesome or criminal characters and depictions of violence. In general, however, most people ignored the criticism, choosing to view comics as harmless fun. But in 1954, the comic book industry was rocked by the publication of *Seduction of the Innocent*. In this book, the respected psychiatrist Fredric Wertham claimed that comics caused juvenile delinquency. *Seduction of the Innocent* sparked an uproar that resulted in a special Senate investigation. All of a sudden, parents and teachers all over the nation began to think of comics as harmful trash. Sales dropped like a stone; many comics companies closed their doors. Even longtime pros like Simon and Kirby found

In the 1950s, concerned parents and lawmakers increasingly criticized comic books for their violent and sexual content. In this 1954 photo, Assemblyman James A. Fitzpatrick of New York *(left)* and Senator Robert C. Hendrickson of New Jersey study a group of typical comic covers. Both men were members of committees studying the effects of comic books on the behavior of American youth.

that there was no work for them. Simon soon left comics for a career in advertising.

Over at Martin Goodman's Atlas Comics, Stan Lee did his best to keep things together. Nevertheless, Atlas struggled along by riding the trends, releasing westerns, teen romances, and giant monster comics. By 1957, however, Super Heroes finally started to make a comeback. At DC, still the biggest comics company, editor Julius Schwartz successfully brought back 1940s heroes including the Flash and Green Lantern. In the new stories, these heroes had science fiction-based powers and different costumes and identities.

Then, toward the end of the 1950s, Schwartz brought out a revolutionary new comic book: *Justice League of America*. The Justice League was a group that featured all of DC's heroes teamed up. It was a huge success. Martin Goodman, ever the trend follower, wanted Stan Lee to create an Atlas super-team to compete with the Justice League. During the rough years, Lee had kept Jack Kirby working, with Kirby cranking out the art for monster comics faster than their stories could be written. So Kirby was the natural choice for artist on Lee's new series. Kirby even had team experience, having worked on his own *Challengers of the Unknown* title while at DC.

The new comic they created, *The Fantastic Four*, was different from other comics. It featured heroes who argued with each other and acted more like real people than any of the heroes who came before. Its debut in November 1961 was a huge hit. As a result, Stan Lee and Jack Kirby began pumping out new Super Hero comic ideas at an amazing rate. This was the beginning of a new era for Martin Goodman's company, which would soon be called Marvel Comics. For the first time in years, DC Comics once again had a serious competitor.

CAP COMES BACK

One of the other new comics that Lee and Kirby developed was a Justice League-style team book. Called *The Avengers*, the book starred all of the duo's most popular characters. These included Iron

Man, the Hulk, Ant-Man, the Wasp, and Thor. Similar to the Fantastic Four, the Avengers did not always get along. But the Avengers lineup was not complete until issue #4 in 1964. For that issue, Stan Lee brought his old friend, Captain America, out of retirement.

To welcome Cap back properly, Jack Kirby drew the story. In it, the Avengers travel to the Arctic following the Sub-Mariner, another Marvel Super Hero. The Sub-Mariner is on a dangerous rampage because the people of his native Atlantis abandoned him. He takes out his anger on the local Inuit people, whom he sees worshipping a human-like figure frozen in a block of ice. Calling the Inuits foolish, the Sub-Mariner throws the block into a local river. As the ice block drifts south, it melts. Luckily, the Avengers discover the figure floating in the freezing water. When they pull it into their submarine, the group is shocked to discover

Captain America joined the Avengers in issue #4, but by issue #16 (above), he was the only Avenger left. In this issue, Cap's leadership skills helped him train new recruits. They included three former villains: the Scarlet Witch; her brother Quicksilver; and Hawkeye, the archer. Cap was one of the most popular Avengers, leading the team for much of its history.

that it is, in fact, Captain America. To explain this surprising turn of events, Lee devised a backstory about Cap's final mission.

In the last days of World War II, the backstory went, Cap and Bucky fought one of their archenemies, Baron Zemo. Zemo launched an experimental drone plane that had been fitted with a bomb. Cap and Bucky jumped on the plane at the last minute. When the bomb exploded in the air, Cap fell into the ocean and Bucky was killed. Cap drifted in the water until the cold temperatures reacted with the

WILL THE REAL CAPTAIN AMERICA PLEASE STAND UP ?

When Marvel brought back Captain America in 1964, Stan Lee simply ignored Cap's 1950s, anti-Communist adventures as if they had never happened. Much later, in 1972, writer Steve Englehart explained what happened to the 1950s Cap. From issues 153 to 156, Englehart and artist Sal Buscema told the story of a young man who discovers a lost formula for the Super-Soldier serum. The man brings the formula to the U.S. government and asks them to make him the new Captain America. First, he undergoes plastic surgery to look like Steve Rogers. Then he rescues an orphan named Jack Monroe, who becomes the new Bucky. The two of them take the serum and begin fighting Communists as Captain America and Bucky.

Unfortunately, they did not know that they needed to be exposed to Vita-Rays for the Super-Soldier process to be complete. Without this final step, the serum begins to drive them both mad. The two eventually go on a destructive rampage against anyone they suspect of being a Communist. As a result, the government has to capture them and place them in suspended animation. When the imposters wake up years later, the real Steve Rogers defeats them.

Super-Soldier serum and left him in a state of suspended animation. He had been stuck there, in a solid block of ice, until Sub-Mariner threw him in the river.

After making sure he is the real thing, the Avengers quickly offer Cap membership in their team. They also promise to help him adjust to life in the early 1960s.

As he did with all of his Marvel characters, Stan Lee gave the new Cap a complex personality. Cap had been totally confident in the old days, but waking up in a new era leaves him confused and sad. He is haunted by guilt over the death of Bucky. In addition, he is unsure of what America means in the 1960s. Readers went wild for this new type of hero with many dimensions and real emotions. Soon Cap was costarring in *Tales of Suspense* with Iron Man. Finally, with issue #100 in 1968, the *Tales of Suspense* title became *Captain America*.

Cap's return in the pages of *The Avengers* in 1964 was a smash success. So, it made sense that Marvel would have him star once again in a book of his own. Before he got his solo title, however, he first costarred with Iron Man in the *Tales of Suspense* series.

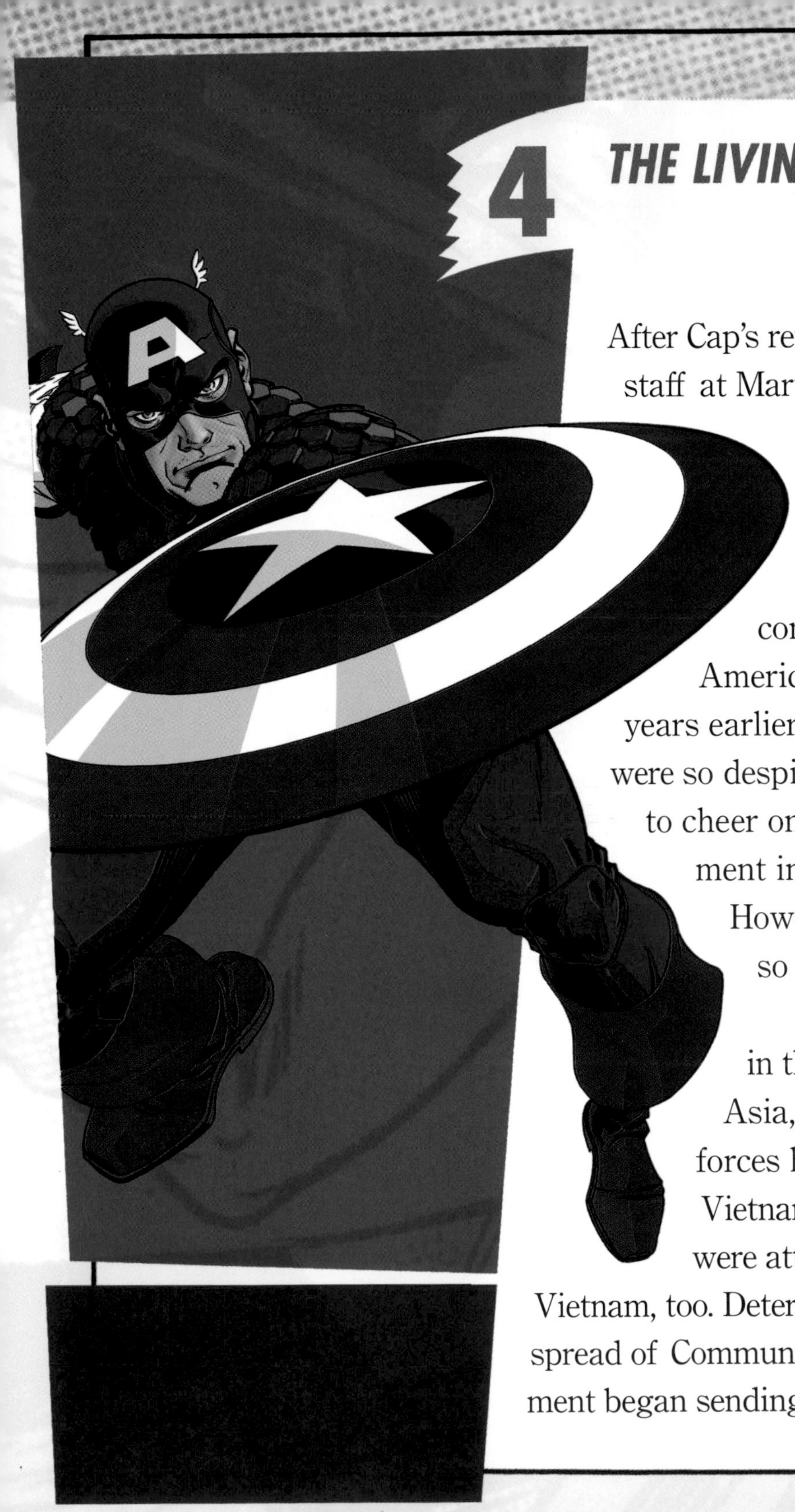

4 THE LIVING LEGEND

After Cap's return, Stan Lee and his staff at Marvel milked the "man-out-of-time" storyline for maximum drama. The 1960s was one of the wildest and most confusing decades in American history. Twenty years earlier, Hitler and the Nazis were so despicable that it was easy to cheer on American involvement in World War II. However, things were not so simple in the 1960s. America was involved in the conflict in Southeast Asia, where Communist forces had seized North Vietnam. The Communists were attempting to take South Vietnam, too. Determined to stop the spread of Communism, the U.S. government began sending troops to the region.

Also during this time, competition with the Soviet Union brought about terrifying new nuclear weapons. Such developments led many Americans to question their government's actions. Marvel's writers used this tension as powerful fuel for *Captain America*'s stories.

CHANGING TIMES

Cap struggled to make sense of the world. People everywhere had new attitudes about civil rights, sexuality, and drug use. Popular music was louder and more experimental than ever. The longhaired hippies who led the antiwar protests were the opposite of the clean-cut young people in the 1940s.

America was divided. Some people thought the Vietnam War was worth fighting, but others felt that peace should be the greatest goal. Cap's attitudes sometimes reflected these real-world conflicts. Cap often worked through S.H.I.E.L.D., a government intelligence organization. And he was partnered up—and romantically linked—with the organization's Agent 13. Even though he had these government ties, Cap regularly bristled at the government's authority.

As the 1960s turned into the 1970s, the conflict in Vietnam was still raging. Young Americans were dying in a war that many opposed. The media regularly showed the results of the horrific violence in Southeast Asia. American soldiers there were accused of brutality and war crimes. For the first time, Americans were not sure if they were really the "good guys." With all of this political turmoil, it was a tough time to be the man with the American flag on his chest.

During World War II, young men voluntarily lined up to fight America's enemies overseas. During the Vietnam War, on the other hand, young American men were generally much less willing to put their lives on the line. Antiwar protesters, like those shown here, began to view the U.S. government as the enemy. This reality was reflected in the new storylines in *Captain America*.

Captain America was starting to look outdated. His sales were declining, and writers were not sure what to do with him. They did try some interesting twists. For instance, Cap was paired with the Falcon, an African American crime fighter. However, *Captain America* was losing steam. Was there a place for Steve Rogers in Vietnam-era America?

CAP QUESTIONS AUTHORITY

In 1972, writer Steve Englehart took over *Captain America* with issue #153. With artist Sal Buscema, Englehart redefined Rogers as a man who believed in the core ideals of America's Constitution, even if that meant going against government orders.

America's spirit took another hit in 1974. That year, President Richard Nixon was forced to resign. Nixon, a Republican, had first been elected president in 1968. He was caught trying to spy on his Democratic rivals in a plot to ensure his reelection in 1972. Many American people were shocked to find out that even the president could be corrupted by power. If the president was a criminal, they asked, then what did that say about the nation he led?

In a memorable Englehart storyline, written to reflect events in the real world, Captain America defeats the fictional "Secret Empire." When Cap finally uncovers the identity of the enemy's "Number One," it is none other than the American president himself. Shocked, Captain America confronts him. Rather than face prison and disgrace, the president commits suicide.

In the issues that followed, starting with #176, a disgusted Steve Rogers is unsure if he still believes in his country. He even gives up his costume and shield. For several issues, he continues fighting crime as the Nomad, a "man without a home." However, he returns to his role as Captain America just in time to fight his old enemy, the Red Skull. Since he no longer trusts the U.S. government, Rogers pledges his loyalty to America's political ideals rather than to America's political leaders.

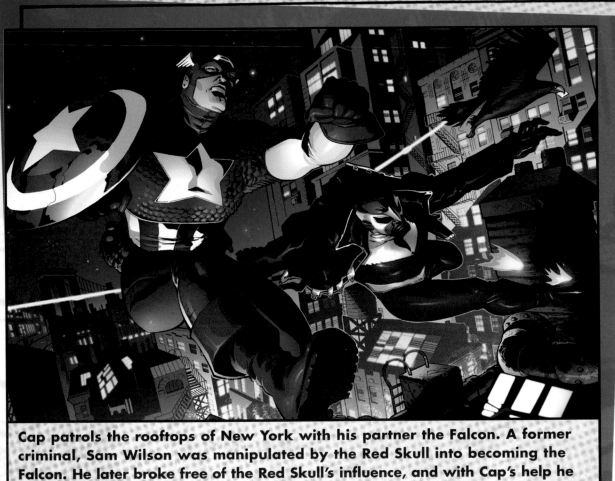

Cap patrols the rooftops of New York with his partner the Falcon. A former criminal, Sam Wilson was manipulated by the Red Skull into becoming the Falcon. He later broke free of the Red Skull's influence, and with Cap's help he became a hero. Falcon is one of comics' most popular and visible African American characters. He has also been a member of the Avengers.

CAP HOLDS STEADY

By the mid-1970s, the American situation was settling down a little. Nixon was gone, and the conflict in Vietnam was coming to an end. When Steve Englehart left *Captain America* to work on other projects, Cap's adventures became less political. At this time, Jack Kirby returned as editor, writer, and artist. He placed Cap in strange science fiction situations where he fought against bizarre enemies. In this way, Cap returned to being more of a classic Super Hero. Also during this time, the Falcon became more popular and got more and more focus in the *Captain America* book. For a period, the title was even changed to *Captain America and the Falcon.*

As the 1970s turned to the 1980s, American attitudes changed yet again. Ronald Reagan was elected president in 1980. He was a firm believer in fighting global Communism. He also thought it was important to strengthen America's nuclear arsenal. The political uncertainty of the Vietnam era was a thing of the past, and a new wave of optimistic patriotism swept the nation.

Reagan had been a film actor for many years before entering politics. In his own life, he showed how popularity in one career could translate into success in American politics. A 1980 storyline by writer Roger Stern and artist John Byrne touched on this concept. Captain America, a great success as a defender of American values, is nominated as a presidential candidate by a third-party group. Ultimately, however, Cap is unable to confine himself to politics and decides not to accept the nomination.

MAKING HIS "MARK"

In 1985, writer Mark Gruenwald began a ten-year run as the writer of *Captain America.* During this period, Steve Rogers abandons the Captain America identity for a second time. The government claims that it owns the Captain America identity and demands that Rogers agree to do its bidding if he is to continue as Captain America.

Rogers refuses and gives up his shield and costume. The government then replaces him with a young man named John Walker.

Walker had been operating as "the Super-Patriot." When he takes over as Captain America, things quickly go wrong. Unlike Steve Rogers, Walker uses brutal and merciless tactics. He even murders two men who reveal his secret identity to the public. Rogers, who had been operating with a new costume as "the Captain," is horrified. For a while, Rogers and Walker are forced to work together against the Red Skull. Afterwards, the government and Walker agree that Rogers should return to take up the Captain America identity. Walker, determined to make up for his sins, continues on as U.S.Agent. The story was Gruenwald's criticism of blindly supporting one's own country. It showed how patriotism without compassion could lead to unnecessary violence.

Also during Gruenwald's run, Captain America fights in the war on drugs. This storyline reflected the epidemic of crack cocaine use that plagued America's inner cities in the 1980s. In one story, Cap is caught in a warehouse explosion that introduces a designer drug into his system. Called Ice, the drug bonds with the Super-Soldier serum in his blood and makes Cap act strangely. The only way to get rid of the Ice is to remove the serum from his blood. Fortunately, Cap eventually gets the clean serum back in his system.

A HERO REBORN

In 1995, after ten years of writing *Captain America*, Mark Gruenwald left the title. The talented writer Mark Waid replaced him, working with artist Ron Garney. Under Waid and Garney, *Captain America* gained some momentum.

Despite the increased interest, however, Marvel pulled the team off of the book to make way for a company-wide "restarting" event. In a long-running crossover with the X-Men, Marvel killed off many of their Super Heroes, including Cap. With everyone dead, Marvel restarted *The Avengers*, *Fantastic Four*, *Iron Man*, and *Captain America* with new #1 issues featuring Jim Lee and Rob Liefeld, comics superstars who were both artists and writers. The new line of comics, called *Heroes Reborn*, was popular enough, but many Captain America fans were angry that Waid and Garney were taken off of the title just as they were hitting their stride.

In the Heroes Reborn universe, Cap was not frozen in ice back in 1945. Instead, he was brainwashed into thinking he was a "normal guy" with a family. When he returns as Cap, his new sidekick is not Bucky but a plucky teenage girl. The book was successful at first, but Liefeld's team was inconsistent. After a while, they were pulled off of the book. Fans were frustrated. They wanted their Cap back. Soon, in another event called Heroes Return, they would get him.

Captain America returned to the Marvel Universe in 1997 with yet another #1 issue. At that time, Mark Waid and Ron Garney came back, too. The book remained popular under Waid, who was soon joined by artist Andy Kubert. When Waid left the title, he was replaced by Dan Jurgens, a former *Superman* writer at DC Comics. This volume of Cap's adventures ran for fifty issues.

Cap made it to the end of the twentieth century intact. He had survived a world war, the Communist threat, nuclear dangers, and the drug war. But in 2001, history once again made Marvel rethink its approach to its most American hero.

A SOBERING REALITY

Terrorists struck at the heart of America on September 11, 2001. In light of this development, in June 2002, *Captain America* was restarted once again with a new #1 issue. The new issues featured stunningly realistic art by John Cassaday and a thought-provoking story by John Ney Reiber. In the most realistic adventures readers had ever seen, Cap was pitted against Islamic terrorists.

Cassaday took pains to make details like the armored scale plating on Cap's jersey look real. Reiber's new stories asked tough questions about the real world: What are the causes of terrorism? What is the best way to honorably defend America? While some were impressed with the new direction, many others did not like seeing Cap so conflicted. After thirty-two issues, Marvel prepared to end the storyline and release yet another #1 issue.

A DEADLY REUNION

In 2004, Captain America returned with new monthly adventures written by Ed Brubaker. These were drawn by artist Steve Epting, who made his name writing dark, intelligent crime comics. The new Captain America series aimed to balance real-world political thrills and classic Super Hero action. Brubaker introduced many controversial elements to the story, including the deaths of the Red Skull and Jack Monroe (the 1950s Bucky).

The most sensational aspect of the new Cap series, however, was the information that Bucky might not have died after all. Instead, he might have been working for a renegade Russian general. Fans hotly debated whether this was a good or bad thing, but it could not be argued that these fresh ideas brought new attention to the series. At over sixty years old, *Captain America* was still able to attract a crowd.

In 2002, when Cap's series was relaunched yet again, artist John Cassaday modernized Cap's uniform, seen here. The highly detailed suit mirrored the increased realism in the storylines. The realistic stories soon returned to more classic storylines, but the illustrations retained Cap's new look.

TIMELINE: JOE SIMON AND JACK KIRBY

1915 November 10: Joe Simon is born in Rochester, New York.

1917 August 28: Jack Kirby is born Jacob Kurtzberg on Essex Street, in New York's Lower East Side.

1939 Kirby lands a salaried position at Fox Features Syndicate. Joe Simon later joins him there.

1940 December: Debut of *Captain America Comics* #1 (cover date March 1941), by Simon and Kirby. The issue, with a cover featuring Captain America knocking out Adolf Hitler, sells a million copies.

1943 Simon and Kirby both enter the military during World War II.

1954 Simon and Kirby found their own company, Mainline Comics. Titles include *Bullseye: Western Scout* and *Foxhole*.

1961 Jack Kirby teams up with Stan Lee for the company soon to be known as Marvel (and formerly known as both Timely and Atlas). Marvel Comics' *Fantastic Four* #1 ushers in the "Marvel Age of Comics," which continues into the twenty-first century.

1969 Simon and Kirby find themselves on opposite sides of a lawsuit when Simon sues for copyright privileges of *Captain America*. Kirby, thinking Simon wants full ownership of the character, sides with Marvel. The relationship between the two men is never the same.

1974 Simon and Kirby team up one more time for the unexpected hit revival of Sandman for DC Comics.

1987 Kirby retires from comics for good.

1994 February 6: Jack Kirby dies. He is laid to rest as perhaps the greatest comic book artist of all time.

CAPTAIN AMERICA HIGHLIGHTS

1941 March: Timely publishes *Captain America Comics* #1 by Joe Simon and Jack Kirby. (First issue hits newstands in December 1940.) Steve Rogers ingests the Super-Soldier serum and becomes Captain America. James Buchanan "Bucky" Barnes becomes his sidekick. Captain America also meets his archenemy, the Red Skull.

1950 The final issue, #75. By this time, Cap is not even the star of the book anymore. It is called *Captain America's Weird Tales* and features horror stories.

1964 *Avengers* #4. Captain America returns in the new Marvel Universe. Fished out of the sea by the Avengers, he is quickly offered membership in their team.

1968 *Captain America* #100. Cap teams up with S.H.I.E.L.D. Agent 13, Sharon Carter, his long-time love interest.

1973 *Captain America* #175. Captain America discovers that the U.S. president is the leader of a criminal conspiracy. Unsure if he can continue representing America, Cap quits.

1987 *Captain America* #332–351. The government replaces Steve Rogers with John Walker. However, after the two team up against the Red Skull, Rogers returns as Captain America.

1996 Captain America, the Avengers, and the Fantastic Four all appear to die in battle against the villain named Onslaught. In truth, they are transported to a parallel universe by Franklin Richards, the young son of Mister Fantastic. Here, Captain America's story restarts.

2002 Another *Captain America* #1, by John Ney Reiber and John Cassaday. Cap fights realistic terrorists.

2004 In yet one more #1 issue, Captain America's archenemy, the Red Skull, is murdered. Cap also runs into the Winter Soldier, a mercenary who may or may not be Cap's old partner, Bucky.

GLOSSARY

archenemy A main or principal enemy.

Communism A form of social organization in which all members of a community share work and property.

conflicted Torn between two different things or ideas.

cover date The date on the cover of a periodical. Comics often appear on newsstands a month or two before their cover date.

exploits Spectacular or heroic actions or adventures.

grunt A U.S. Army foot soldier.

invulnerable Unable to be hurt or harmed.

juvenile delinquency Conduct by a young person that society considers offensive and is sometimes illegal.

patriotism A feeling of pride in one's own country.

pseudonym A false name used in place of an author's or artist's real name.

serum A potion or liquid medicine.

suspended animation A state in which a person seems to lose vital functions. Unlike in death, someone in suspended animation can be brought back to an animated state.

turmoil An unsettled state.

tyrant Someone, usually a ruler, who exercises power brutally.

unwholesome Not respectable or honorable.

The Jack Kirby Museum and Research Center
828 Bloomfield Street, #3
Hoboken, NJ 07030
(201) 963-4383
Web site: http://www.kirbymuseum.org

Museum of Comic and Cartoon Art
594 Broadway, Suite 401
New York, NY 10012
(212) 254-3511
Web site: http://www.moccany.org

WEB SITES

Due to the changing nature of Internet links, the Rosen Publishing Group, Inc., has developed an online list of Web sites related to the subject of this book. The site is updated regularly. Please use this link to access the list:

http://www.rosenlinks.com/crah/caam

You can also refer to Marvel's Web site:

http://www.marvel.com

FOR FURTHER READING

Brubaker, Ed, and Steve Epting. *Captain America: The Winter Soldier*, Vol. 1. New York, NY: Marvel Comics, 2005.

Daniels, Les. *Marvel: Five Fabulous Decades of the World's Greatest Comics.* New York, NY: Harry N. Abrams, Inc., 1991.

Englehart, Steve, Sal Buscema, and Mike Friedrich. *Captain America and the Falcon: Secret Empire.* New York, NY: Marvel Comics, 2006.

Gruenwald, Mark, and Ron Lim. *Captain America: Streets of Poison.* New York, NY: Marvel Comics, 1994.

Jones, Gerard. *Men of Tomorrow: Geeks, Gangsters, and the Birth of the Comic Book.* New York, NY: Basic Books, 2004.

Kirby, Jack. *Captain America: Madbomb.* New York, NY: Marvel Comics, 2004.

Kirby, Jack. *Captain America and the Falcon: Bicentennial Battles.* New York, NY: Marvel Comics, 2005.

Lee, Stan, and Jack Kirby. *The Essential Captain America*, Vol. 1. New York, NY: Marvel Comics, 2000.

Lee, Stan, and various artists. *The Essential Captain America*, Vol. 2. New York, NY: Marvel Comics, 2002.

Lee, Stan, Don Heck, and Jack Kirby. *The Essential Avengers*, Vol. 1. New York, NY: Marvel Comics, 1998.

Morales, Robert, and Kyle Baker. *Truth: Red, White, and Black.* New York, NY: Marvel Comics, 2004.

Rieber, John Ney, and John Cassaday. *Captain America: The New Deal.* New York, NY: Marvel Comics, 2003.

Ro, Ronin. *Tales to Astonish: Jack Kirby, Stan Lee, and the American Comic Book Revolution.* New York, NY: Bloomsbury, 2004.

Sanderson, Peter. *Marvel Universe.* New York, NY: Harry N. Abrams, 1996.

Simon, Joe, and Jack Kirby. *Captain America: The Classic Years,* Vol. 1. New York, NY: Marvel Comics, 1998.

Simon, Joe, and Jack Kirby. *Captain America: The Classic Years,* Vol. 2. New York, NY: Marvel Comics, 2000.

Simon, Joe, and Jim Simon. *The Comic Book Makers.* New York, NY: Crestwood Publications, 1990.

Stern, Roger, and John Byrne. *Captain America: War and Remembrance.* New York, NY: Marvel Comics, 1991.

Waid, Mark, and Ron Garney. *Captain America: Man Without a Country.* New York, NY: Marvel Comics, 1998.

Waid, Mark, and Ron Garney. *Captain America: Operation: Rebirth.* New York, NY: Marvel Comics, 1996.

BIBLIOGRAPHY

Daniels, Les. *Marvel: Five Fabulous Decades of the World's Greatest Comics*. New York, NY: Harry N. Abrams, Inc., 1991

Evanier, Mark, and Steve Sherman. "Jack Kirby Biography." The Jack Kirby Museum and Research Center. Retrieved September 10, 2005 (http://www.kirbymuseum.org/biography.html).

Jones, Gerard. *Men of Tomorrow: Geeks, Gangsters, and the Birth of the Comic Book*. New York, NY: Basic Books, 2004.

Lee, Stan, Don Heck, and Jack Kirby. *The Essential Avengers*, Vol. 1. New York, NY: Marvel Comics, 1998.

Ro, Ronin. *Tales to Astonish: Jack Kirby, Stan Lee, and the American Comic Book Revolution*. New York, NY: Bloomsbury, 2004.

Sanderson, Peter. *Marvel Universe*. New York, NY: Harry N. Abrams, 1996.

Simon, Joe, and Jim Simon. *The Comic Book Makers*. New York, NY: Crestwood Publications, 1990.

INDEX

B

Brubaker, Ed, 38, 39
Bucky, 19, 22, 28, 29, 37, 39
Buscema, Sal, 28, 33

C

Captain America
    explanation for anti-Communist
        stories, 28
    1964 comeback, 27, 28
    as the Nomad, 33
    origin of, 18–19
    premiere of, 16–18, 20
    replaced by John Walker, 36
    series cancelled, 22, 24
    series restarted, 37, 38
    shield of, 19, 36
Cassaday, John, 38
Communism, 23, 30, 35, 38

E

Englehart, Steve, 28, 33, 34
Epting, Steve, 38

F

Falcon, the, 32, 35
Fantastic Four, The, 26, 37

G

Garney, Ron, 37
Golden Girl, 22
Goodman, Martin, 13, 14, 16, 19, 21,
    25, 26

Great Depression, 6
Gruenwald, Mark, 35, 36

H

Hitler, Adolf, 15, 16, 18, 30

J

Jurgens, Dan, 37

K

Kirby, Jack (Jacob Kurtzberg)
    and DC Comics, 21
    early life of, 6, 7–8, 12
    in the military, 21
    names of, 7, 11, 14
Kubert, Andy, 37

L

Lee, Jim, 37
Lee, Stan, 21, 22, 23, 24, 25, 26–27, 28, 29, 30
Liefeld, Rob, 37

N

Nixon, Richard, 33, 34

R

Reagan, Ronald, 35
Red Skull, the, 20, 33, 36, 39
Reiber, John Ney, 38
Romita, John, 24

S

Shield, the, 19

Simon, Joe
    career change to advertising, 25
    and DC Comics, 21
    early life of, 6, 12
    in the military, 21
Superman, 10–11, 13, 14, 18, 20, 37

T

terrorism, 38

V

Vietnam, 30, 31–32, 34, 35
Vision, the, 14

W

Waid, Mark, 36–37
World War II, 15–16, 20, 21, 22, 23,
    28, 30

ABOUT THE AUTHOR

Thomas Forget is a lifelong comic book fan and former Marvel Comics editorial intern. He has previously written books on pop-culture subjects as diverse as zombie films, the Beastie Boys, and graphic novelist Art Spiegelman. He lives in Brooklyn, where Captain America also currently has his secret headquarters.

PHOTO CREDITS

p. 9 courtesy of the Kirby Estate and *Jack Kirby Collector* magazine (www.twomorrows.com) © Kirby Estate; p. 10 Library of Congress Prints and Photographs Division © King Features Syndicate; p. 12 © Betty Sinnott courtesy of the Sinnott family; pp. 25, 32 © Bettmann/Corbis. All other images provided by Marvel Entertainment, Inc.

Designer: Thomas Forget
Editor: Christopher Roberts
Photo Researcher: Les Kanturek